The Jane Austen Dictionary

A Collection of Useful and Interesting Words
from Austen's Works

Emmalee Haskell

DEDICATION

For M. B., who taught me how to write; for the wonderful A. C., whose participants are generous both with their encouragement and with good advice; above all, for D. R. H., who answered a thousand questions and who always thinks I can.

ACKNOWLEDGMENTS

This book could not exist without the dutiful spirit of record-keeping
exhibited by those who lived and worked during the eighteenth and
nineteenth centuries. Instruction books on sailing and seamanship;
early English dictionaries and translation enchiridia; cookbooks; and
so forth formed the knowledge base from which the word definitions
herein were created. All materials drawn from were original texts
from the relevant time period. No copyrighted works were used in
the making of this dictionary.

Great thanks must also be given to my baby, for napping whilst this
book was written.

A

Ablution *noun*   The act of cleansing.

"'Mr. Darcy may perhaps have heard of such a place as Gracechurch Street, but he would hardly think a month's ablution enough to cleanse him from its impurities, were he once to enter it; and depend upon it, Mr. Bingley never stirs without him.'"
—*Pride & Prejudice* chapter XXV

Abstruse *adjective*   Difficult; obscure; requiring work to understand.

"'But I had no inclination for the law, even in this less abstruse study of it, which my family approved.'"
—*Sense & Sensibility* chapter XIX

Accede *verb*   Assent; agree.

" . . . as Mrs. Elton had very readily acceded to it, so it was to be, if she had no objection."

—Emma volume I chapter VI

". . . Fanny would rather not have been asked; but it was impossible for her to refuse the correspondence; it was impossible for her even not to accede to it more readily than her own judgment authorised."

—Mansfield Park chapter XXXVI

Accession *noun*   Enlargement; increase.

"Emma spoke her pity so very kindly, that with a sudden accession of gay thought, he cried, 'Ah! by the bye,' then sinking his voice, and looking demure for the moment—'I hope Mr. Knightley is well?'"

—Emma volume III chapter XVIII

"Fanny's spirits lived on it half the morning, deriving some accession of pleasure from its writer being himself to go away."

—Mansfield Park chapter XXVII

Ague *noun*   An intermitting fever, with cold fits followed by heat.

". . . for she had set him right as to his grandson's illness, convinced him that it was an ague, and promised him a charm for it . . ."

—Mansfield Park chapter X

Acrimony *noun*   Sharpness; corrosiveness.

"It was gratitude; gratitude, not merely for having once loved her, but for loving her still well enough to forgive all the petulance and acrimony of her manner in rejecting him, and all the unjust accusations accompanying her rejection."

—*Pride & Prejudice* chapter XLIV

Alacrity *noun*   Sprightliness.

"Lucy directly drew her work table near her and reseated herself with an alacrity and cheerfulness which seemed to infer that she could taste no greater delight than in making a filigree basket for a spoilt child."

—*Sense & Sensibility* chapter XXIII

Allay *verb*   Pacify; make quiet; soothe.

"The tumult of Elizabeth's mind was allayed by this conversation."

—*Pride & Prejudice* chapter XL

"The ladies knew better how to allay it. Mr. Weston must be quiet, and every thing deliberately arranged."

—*Emma* volume II chapter VII

"They were of sobering tendency; they allayed agitation; they composed, and consequently must make her happier."

—*Persuasion* chapter VII

Amiable *adjective*   Lovable; inspiring love; worthy to be loved.

"She had reached the age of seventeen, without having seen one amiable youth who could call forth her sensibility, without having inspired one real passion, and without having excited even any admiration but what was very moderate and very transient."

—*Northanger Abbey* chapter I

"'I cannot be otherwise than concerned at being the means of injuring your amiable daughters, and beg leave to apologise for it, as well as to assure you of my readiness to make them every possible amends . . .'"

—*Pride & Prejudice* chapter XIII

Apoplexy *noun*   A sudden loss of all sensation.

"They lived together; and when Dr. Grant had brought on apoplexy and death, by three great institutionary dinners in one week, they still lived together."

—*Mansfield Park* chapter XLVIII

Appertaining *adjective* Rightly or naturally belonging to.

"Mr. Yates had staid to see the destruction of every theatrical preparation at Mansfield, the removal of everything appertaining to the play."

—*Mansfield Park* chapter XX

Approbation *noun*   Approval; support; liking.

"The next meeting of the two Mansfield families produced another alteration in the plan, and one that was admitted with general approbation."

—Mansfield Park chapter VIII

". . . if his consent and approbation could be obtained—which, she trusted, would be attended with no difficulty, since it was a plan to promote the happiness of all—she and Mr. Knightley meant to marry . . ."

—Emma volume III chapter XVII

Arrant, errant *adjective*   Extremely bad; horrible.

"'Nonsense, arrant nonsense, as ever was talked!' cried Mr. Knightley."

—Emma volume I chapter VIII

Asperity *adjective*   Roughness or ruggedness.

"But he was set right there by Mrs. Bennet, who assured him with some asperity that they were very well able to keep a good cook, and that her daughters had nothing to do in the kitchen."

—Pride & Prejudice chapter XIII

"'Not Harriet's equal!' exclaimed Mr. Knightley loudly and warmly; and with calmer asperity, added, a few moments afterwards, 'No, he is not her equal indeed, for he is as much her superior in sense as in situation.'"

—Emma volume I, chapter VIII

Assiduously *adverb*   Constantly; continuously; diligently.

"". . . in your heart, you thoroughly despised the persons who so assiduously courted you.""

—*Pride & Prejudice* chapter LX

"While Sir Walter and Elizabeth were assiduously pushing their good fortune in Laura Place, Anne was renewing an acquaintance of a very different description."

—*Persuasion* chapter XVII

B

Beaufet *noun*   A type of table or cupboard furniture, or the party refreshments arranged thereon.

". . . almost ready to overpower them with care and kindness, thanks for their visit, solicitude for their shoes, anxious inquiries after Mr. Woodhouse's health, cheerful communications about her mother's, and sweet-cake from the beaufet . . ."

—Emma volume II, Chapter I

Beneficence *noun*   Active kindness characterized by doing good.

"". . . the Right Honourable Lady Catherine de Bourgh, widow of Sir Lewis de Bourgh, whose bounty and beneficence has preferred me to the valuable rectory of this parish . . .""

—Pride & Prejudice chapter XIII

Blackguard *noun*   A dirty fellow. (Probably originating from the word denoting a servant in a great house whose duties included carrying coal.)

"'I am shut out for ever from their society, they already think me an unprincipled fellow, this letter will only make them think me a blackguard one.'"

—*Sense & Sensibility* chapter XLIV

Bon mot *noun*   Joke; witticism; clever saying. (French.)

"'You need not hurry when the object is only to prevent my saying a *bon mot*, for there is not the least wit in my nature. I am a very matter-of-fact, plain-spoken being, and may blunder on the borders of a repartee for half an hour together without striking it out.'"

—*Mansfield Park* chapter IX

Bon vivant *noun*   A jolly fellow; a person who lives in a luxurious fashion. (French.) From "bon" (well) and "vivant" (living).

"'. . . I see him to be an indolent, selfish *bon vivant*, who must have his palate consulted in everything; who will not stir a finger for the convenience of any one . . .'"

—*Mansfield Park* chapter XI

C

Cadet *noun*   The younger or youngest son.

"'Bertram is certainly well off for a cadet of even a baronet's family.'"

—*Mansfield Park* chapter XXIII

Cant *noun*   1. Speech in a lower-class dialect. 2. Jargon belonging to a particular profession. 3. Anything said pretentiously or in affectation. 4. Silly chatter; a common expression, usually applied with little meaning.

". . . her face was so lovely, that when in the common cant of praise, she was called a beautiful girl, truth was less violently outraged than usually happens."

—*Sense & Sensibility* chapter X

Canvass *verb*   1. Examine; consider. 2. Debate.

"The subject which had been so warmly canvassed between their parents, about a twelvemonth ago, was now brought forward again."

—Pride & Prejudice chapter LIII

"'We think so very differently on this point, Mr. Knightley, that there can be no use in canvassing it.'"

—Emma volume I chapter VIII

Captiously *adverb*　　In a manner that is characterized by an inclination to object; in way that displays eagerness to oppose.

"'We are not boy and girl, to be captiously irritable, misled by every moment's inadvertence, and wantonly playing with our own happiness.'"

—Persuasion chapter XXII

Cavil *verb*　　Raise captious and frivolous objections.

"Anne, far from wishing to cavil at the pleasure, replied, 'I can easily believe it.'"

—Persuasion chapter XVII

Caviller *noun*　　An unfair adversary; a captious disputant; a person who cavils (i.e., raises captious and frivolous objections).

"'For my temptation to think it a right, I refer every caviller to a brick house, sashed windows below, and casements above, in Highbury.'"

—Emma volume III, chapter XIV

Celerity *noun*   Swiftness.

"'I dare say you believed it; but I am by no means convinced that you would be gone with such celerity.'"

—Pride & Prejudice chapter X

Cockade *noun*   A ribbon worn in the hat.

"'I took him as he was sleeping on the sofa, and it is as strong a likeness of his cockade as you would wish to see.'"

—Emma volume I chapter VI

Complaisance *noun*   Civility; desire to please.

"'Did I imitate your forbearance, or lessen your restraints, by taking any part in those offices of general complaisance or particular gratitude which you had hitherto been left to discharge alone?'"

—Sense & Sensibility chapter XLVI

"'. . . she was as near giving it up, out of nonsensical complaisance!'"

—Persuasion chapter X

Connubial *adjective*   Matrimonial; nuptial; pertaining to marriage.

"But no such happy marriage could now teach the admiring multitude what connubial felicity really was."

—*Pride & Prejudice* chapter L

Contrariety *noun*   1. Repugnance; opposition. 2. Inconsistency or variety.

". . . it may well be supposed how eagerly she went through them, and what a contrariety of emotion they excited."

—*Pride & Prejudice* chapter XXXVI

Controverted *verb*   Discussed or debated.

". . . she was not used to have her judgment controverted."

—*Pride & Prejudice* chapter XXIX

Convivial *adjective*   1. Festal or celebratory; 2. social.

"Mr. Weston was chatty and convivial, and no friend to early separations of any sort . . ."

—*Emma* volume I chapter XV

Coppice-wood *noun*   Low wood cut at a certain growth for fuel; a place overgrown with short wood. (Also known as a "coppice" or "copse," the latter being an abbreviation which eventually replaced "coppice" altogether.)

"... the valley, here contracted into a glen, allowed room only for the stream, and a narrow walk amidst the rough coppice-wood which bordered it."

—Pride & Prejudice chapter XLIII

Court-baron *noun*   A court incident to ever manor in the kingdom, run by the manor's steward.

"... ancient manorial residence of the family, with all its rights of court-leet and court-baron."

—Mansfield Park chapter VIII

Court-leet *noun*   A court of record, held annually within a particular manor, canton, community, etc. before the steward of the leet. Compound of "court" and "leet," the latter meaning "law-day."

"... ancient manorial residence of the family, with all its rights of court-leet and court-baron."

—Mansfield Park chapter VIII

Coxcomb *noun*   A superficial pretender.

"'A great coxcomb!' repeated Miss Steele, whose ear had caught those words by a sudden pause in Marianne's music. 'Oh, they are talking of their favourite beaux, I daresay.'"

—Sense & Sensibility chapter XXIV

D

Deedily *adjective*   Busily; intently. (Related to the adjective "deedy," meaning "painstaking," "earnest," industrious," or "active.")

"The appearance of the little sitting-room as they entered, was tranquillity itself; Mrs. Bates, deprived of her usual employment, slumbering on one side of the fire, Frank Churchill, at a table near her, most deedily occupied about her spectacles, and Jane Fairfax, standing with her back to them, intent on her pianoforte."

—*Emma* volume II chapter X

Debar *verb*   Exclude; prevent.

"'Could we be all assembled, our satisfaction would undoubtedly be more complete, but the absence of some is not to debar the others of amusement.'"

—*Mansfield Park* chapter XXXVI

Demesnes, demains *noun*   The land adjacent to and belonging with a house.

". . . by walking fifty yards from the hall door, she could look down the park, and command a view of the Parsonage and all its demesnes, gently rising beyond the village road . . ."
>   —*Mansfield Park* chapter VII

"A small green court was the whole of its demesne in front; and a neat wicket gate admitted them into it."
>   —*Sense & Sensibility* chapter VI

Despatch *noun*   Hasty execution.

"*He*, meanwhile, whatever he might feel, acted with all the firmness of a collected mind, made every necessary arrangement with the utmost despatch, and calculated with exactness the time in which she might look for his return."
>   —*Sense & Sensibility* chapter XLIII

". . . one gentleman only was standing there, and it is probable that Elinor was not without hope of exciting his politeness to a quicker dispatch."
>   —*Sense & Sensibility* chapter XXXIII

Desultory *adjective*   Roving from thing to thing; unsettled; immethodical.

"Miss Bates had just done as Patty opened the door; and her visitors walked upstairs without having any regular narration to

attend to, pursued only by the sounds of her desultory good-will."
—*Emma* volume II, chapter IX

Dilatory *adjective*   Tardy; prone to procrastination.

"His letter was soon dispatched; for, though dilatory in undertaking business, he was quick in its execution."
—*Pride & Prejudice* chapter XLVIII

Discomfit *verb*   Defeat; conquer; overthrow.

"But, though discomfited and disappointed, he could still do something for his own interest and his own enjoyment."
—*Persuasion* chapter XXIV

Dissemble *verb*   Hide something under false appearance; conceal; pretend that not to be which really is.

"'But in this, our last interview of friendship, I approached her with a sense of guilt that almost took from me the power of dissembling.'"
—*Sense & Sensibility* chapter XLIV

"'You can hardly doubt the purport of my discourse, however your natural delicacy may lead you to dissemble; my attentions have been too marked to be mistaken.'"
—*Pride & Prejudice* chapter XIX

Doge *noun*   The title of the chief magistrate of Venice and Genoa.

"''To say the truth,' replied Miss Crawford, 'I am something like the famous Doge at the court of Lewis XIV, and may declare that I see no wonder in this shrubbery equal to seeing myself in it.'''
—*Mansfield Park* chapter XXII

Douceur *noun*   Flattery; a lure; a coaxing temptation.

"The impertinence of these kind of scrutinies, moreover, was generally concluded with a compliment, which though meant as its douceur, was considered by Marianne as the greatest impertinence of all . . ."
—*Sense & Sensibility* chapter XXXVI

Dray *noun*   A cart carrying beer.

". . . amidst the dash of other carriages, the heavy rumble of carts and drays, the bawling of newspapermen, muffin-men and milkmen, and the ceaseless clink of pattens . . ."
—*Persuasion* chapter XIV

Dressy *adjective*   Distinguished by dress.

"'I should think he must be rather a dressy man for his time of life. Such a number of looking-glasses!'"
—*Persuasion* chapter XIII

Ductility *noun*   Flexibility; compliance.

"Bingley was endeared to Darcy by the easiness, openness, and ductility of his temper, though no disposition could offer a greater contrast to his own, and though with his own he never appeared dissatisfied."

—*Pride & Prejudice* chapter IV

Duenna *noun*   An old woman hired to guard a young woman.

"'My sister . . . hopes to be admitted into the company, and will be happy to take the part of any old duenna or tame confidante, that you may not like to do yourselves.'"

—*Mansfield Park* chapter XIII

E

Ebullition *noun*   .A bursting forth; a spontaneous expression of high spirits or strong emotions. (A metaphor taken from the sciences, in which it is a word for boiling or expansion of something in a liquid state.)

"'Aye, aye, the parsonage is but a small one,' said she, after the first ebullition of surprise and satisfaction was over . . .'"

—*Sense & Sensibility* chapter XL

Éclaircissement *noun* Explanation; clearing-up. (French.)

"Mr. Rushworth had set off early with the great news for Sotherton; and she had fondly hoped for such an immediate *éclaircissement* as might save him the trouble of ever coming back again."

—*Mansfield Park* chapter XX

Éclat *noun* Splendor; luster; showiness. (French.)

"'We are each of an unsocial, taciturn disposition, unwilling to speak, unless we expect to say something that will amaze the whole room, and be handed down to posterity with all the *éclat* of a proverb.'"

—*Pride & Prejudice* chapter XVIII

"Here too, Miss Dashwood's commendation, being only simple and just, came in without any *éclat.*"

—*Sense & Sensibility* chapter XXI

Elucidation *noun* Explanation; exposition; illustration.

"'This seems to have been a day of general elucidation, for this very morning first unfolded it to us.'"

—*Sense & Sensibility* chapter XXX

Embrocation *noun* A medicinal lotion used for rubbing diseased parts.

"'Either bathing has been of the greatest service to her, or else it is to be attributed to an excellent embrocation of Mr. Wingfield's, which we have been applying at times ever since August.'"

—*Emma* volume I chapter XII

Emendation *noun* Correction.

"Every emendation of Anne's had been on the side of
honesty against importance."

—Persuasion chapter II

Espalier *noun*   Trees grown and cut so as to join.

"She went, however; and when they reached the farm, and
she was to be put down, at the end of the broad, neat gravel walk,
which led between espalier apple-trees to the front door, the sight of
every thing which had given her so much pleasure the autumn
before, was beginning to revive a little local agitation."

—Emma volume II chapter V

Esquire *noun*   A gentlemen of the rank just below the
rank of knight. ("Squire" is simply a contraction of this word. In
earlier times, this word denoted a knight's attendant; by Austen's
time, however, that meaning was out of use.)

"'It will be but the loss of the Esquire after his name.'"

—Mansfield Park chapter V

Evanescent *adjective*   Vanishing or imperceptible.

"'I am afraid I am not quite so much the man of the world as
might be good for me in some points. My feelings are not quite so
evanescent, nor my memory of the past under such an easy dominion
as one finds to be the case with men of the world.'"

—Mansfield Park chapter X

Evince *verb*   Prove; give evidence of.

". . . his mother, who equally heard the conversation which passed at table, did not evince the least disapprobation."
           —*Mansfield Park* chapter XIII

Excursive *adjective*   Rambling; wandering.

"In one of these excursive glances she perceived among a group of young men, the very he, who had given them a lecture on toothpick-cases at Gray's."
         —*Sense & Sensibility* chapter XXXVI

Exigeant *adjective*   Exacting; demanding. (French.)

"'She could not do otherwise than accept him, for he was rich, and she had nothing; but he turns out ill-tempered and *exigeant*, and wants a young woman, a beautiful young woman of five-and-twenty, to be as steady as himself.'"
         —*Mansfield Park* chapter XXXVI

Exigence *noun*   Necessity; need; demand.

"One consolation however remained for them, to which the exigence of the moment gave more than usual propriety; it was that of running with all possible speed down the steep side of the hill which led immediately to their garden gate."
         —*Sense & Sensibility* chapter IX

"'In such exigence, my uncle's advice and assistance would everything in the world . . .'"

—Pride & Prejudice chapter XLVI

Expatiate *verb*   To range at large; to rove without any prescribed limits.

"'I will not reason here—nor will I stop for *you* to expatiate on the absurdity, and the worse than absurdity, of scrupling to engage my faith where my honour was already bound.'"

—Sense & Sensibility chapter XLIV

Expeditious *adjective*   Speedy, quick.

". . . Mr. Palmer, travelling more expeditiously with Colonel Brandon, was to join them . . ."

—Sense & Sensibility chapter XLII

"'Our coachmen and horses are so extremely expeditious!'"

—Emma volume III chapter II

Expensive *adjective*   Prone to extravagance.

"'. . . I had always been expensive, always in the habit of associating with people of better income than myself.'"

—Sense & Sensibility chapter XLIV

"'. . . a mere pretty, silly, expensive, fashionable woman, I believe . . .'"

Expiation *noun*   Removal of guilt.

"'Pain is no expiation.'"

—*Emma* volume III chapter XII

Expostulation *noun*   1. Debate; altercation. 2. Accusation; charge.

"Miss Bingley warmly resented the indignity he had received, in an expostulation with her brother for talking such nonsense."

—*Pride & Prejudice* chapter X

Extant *adjective*   Prominent; protruding; standing out. (Here appearing to carry the meaning "expressive of" or "manifested in.")

". . . some few of the thousand poetical descriptions extant of autumn, that season of peculiar and inexhaustible influence on the mind of taste and tenderness . . ."

—*Persuasion* chapter X

F

Filial *adjective*   1. Pertaining to sonship. 2. Befitting a son.

"'He does seem to have had some filial scruples on that head, as you will hear.'"

—*Pride & Prejudice* chapter XIII

Fracas *noun*   Disturbance; disruption; kerfuffle.

"Fanny read to herself that 'it was with infinite concern the newspaper had to announce to the world a matrimonial fracas in the family of Mr. R. of Wimpole Street.'"

—*Mansfield Park* chapter XLVI

Fricassee *noun*   A dish made of meat, usually chicken, cut into small pieces and dressed with a strong sauce. (French.)

"'. . . there was a delicate *fricassee* of sweetbread and some asparagus brought in at first, and good Mr. Woodhouse, not thinking the asparagus quite boiled enough, sent it all out again.'"

—Emma volume III chapter II

Furlong *noun*   One eighth of a mile.

"'Oh! I know nothing of your furlongs, but I am sure it is a very long wood, and that we have been winding in and out ever since we came into it; and therefore, when I say that we have walked a mile in it, I must speak within compass.'"

—Mansfield Park chapter IX

G

Gad *verb* Ramble without purpose; idly rove.

"'Mrs. Musgrove thinks all her servants so steady, that it would be high treason to call it in question; but I am sure, without exaggeration, that her upper house-maid and laundry-maid, instead of being in their business, are gadding about the village, all day long.'"
—*Persuasion* chapter VI

Gaucherie *noun* Clumsiness or self-consciousness. (French.)

". . . for, talking of his brother, and lamenting the extreme *gaucherie* which he really believed kept him from mixing in proper society, he candidly and generously attributed it much less to any natural deficiency, than to the misfortune of a private education."
—*Sense & Sensibility* chapter XXXVI

Glebe *noun*   The land belonging to a clergyman as part of the benefit of his ecclesiastical position.

"But so little interest had he taken in the matter, that he owed all his knowledge of the house, garden, and glebe, extent of the parish, condition of the land, and rate of the tithes, to Elinor herself . . ."

—*Sense & Sensibility* chapter XLIX

Greensward *noun*   Grassy turf.

"About half a mile beyond Highbury, making a sudden turn, and deeply shaded by elms on each side, it became for a considerable stretch very retired; and when the young ladies had advanced some way into it, they had suddenly perceived at a small distance before them, on a broader patch of greensward by the side, a party of gipsies."

—*Emma* volume III chapter III

H

Hartshorn *noun*   A medicine made from ground stag antlers.

"Marianne was in a silent agony, too much oppressed even for tears; but as Mrs. Jennings was luckily not come home, they could go directly to their own room, where hartshorn restored her a little to herself."

—*Sense & Sensibility* chapter XXVIII

Heterogeneous *adjective*   Dissimilar; diverse.

"'The preacher who can touch and affect such an heterogeneous mass of hearers . . .'"

—*Mansfield Park* chapter XXXIV

I

Importune *verb*   Harass with slight but continually occurring vexations.

"'But I will no longer importune my young cousin.'"
—*Pride & Prejudice* chapter XIV

Ineffable *adjective*   Inexpressible.

"'. . . attending with such ineffable sweetness and patience to all the demands of her aunt's stupidity . . .'"
—*Mansfield Park* chapter XXX

Indubitable *adjective*   Undisputed; unquestionable.

"'That she is a gentleman's daughter, is indubitable to me; that she associates with gentlemen's daughters, no one, I apprehend, will deny.'"

—*Emma* volume I chapter VIII

Inimical *adjective*   Hostile; unfavorable; adverse; opposed.

". . . neither was there anything among the other component parts of the cottage inimical to comfort."

Persuasion chapter VI

Innoxious *adjective*   Pure, free from crime or mischief.

"Everybody has their taste in noises as well as in other matters; and sounds are quite innoxious, or most distressing, by their sort rather than their quantity."

—*Persuasion* chapter XIV

Inure, enure *verb*   Habituate; accustom.

"'By remaining in the neighbourhood, I am become inured to it.'"

—*Persuasion* chapter XIII

"'A younger son, you know, must be inured to self-denial and dependence.'"

—*Persuasion* chapter XXIV

L

Landaulette *noun*   A small carriage, the top of which may be opened. (Diminutive of "landau," a type of carriage the top of which may be opened.)

"She had something to suffer, perhaps, when they came into contact again, in seeing Anne restored to the rights of seniority, and the mistress of a very pretty landaulette; but she had a future to look forward to, of powerful consolation."

—Persuasion chapter XXIV

M

Mien *noun*   Air; look; manner.

"His brother-in-law, Mr. Hurst, merely looked the gentleman; but his friend Mr. Darcy soon drew the attention of the room by his fine, tall person, handsome features, noble mien, and the report which was in general circulation within five minutes after his entrance, of his having ten thousand a year."

—Pride & Prejudice chapter III

Mischance *noun*   Misfortune; misadventure.

"She felt all the perverseness of the mischance that should bring him where no one else was brought, and, to prevent its ever happening again, took care to inform him at first that it was a favourite haunt of hers."

—Pride & Prejudice chapter XXXIII

Missish *adjective*   Characterized by some negative trait considered to be associated with young girlhood (e.g., silliness or over-sensitivity).

"'You are not going to be missish, I hope, and pretend to be affronted by an idle report.'"
—Pride & Prejudice chapter LVII

Mizzle *verb*   Release a small, misty downpour. (A portmanteau of the words "mist" and "drizzle.")

"'Ever since the day—about four years ago—that Miss Taylor and I met with him in Broadway Lane, when, because it began to mizzle, he darted away with so much gallantry, and borrowed two umbrellas for us from Farmer Mitchell's, I made up my mind on the subject.'"
—Emma volume I chapter I

Mohr *noun*   A type of gold coin minted in Calcutta and used as currency in the British East Indies. (Also called a "mohur" or "gold rupee.")

"'Perhaps,' said Willoughby, 'his observations may have extended to the existence of nabobs, gold mohrs, and palanquins.'"
—Sense & Sensibility chapter X

Moiety *noun*   Half; one of two equal parts.

"Their mother had nothing, and their father only seven thousand pounds in his own disposal; for the remaining moiety of his

first wife's fortune was also secured to her child, and he had only a
life-interest in it."

—Sense & Sensibility chapter I

N

Nabob *noun*   An Indian prince.

"'Perhaps,' said Willoughby, 'his observations may have extended to the existence of nabobs, gold mohrs, and palanquins.'"
—*Sense & Sensibility* chapter X

Negus *noun*   A drink made with wine, oranges, and lemon juice.

". . . feverish with hopes and fears, soup and negus, sore-footed and fatigued, restless and agitated, yet feeling, in spite of everything, that a ball was indeed delightful."
—*Mansfield Park* chapter XXVIII

Novitiate *noun*   1. The condition or status of being a novice. 2. A person who is learning the rudiments of a subject.

"With the fortitude of a devoted novitiate, she had resolved at one-and-twenty to complete the sacrifice, and retire from all the pleasures of life, of rational intercourse, equal society, peace and hope, to penance and mortification for ever."

—Emma volume II chapter II

Nuncheon *noun* Midday meal. ("Nuncheon" likely originated from the word "noon" and "schenche," meaning "drink"; as it came to denote a meal rather than simply a drink, the word "lump," as in "lump of bread," was added, giving rise to the word "luncheon.")

"'I left London this morning at eight o'clock, and the only ten minutes I have spent out of my chaise since that time procured me a nuncheon at Marlborough.'"

—Sense & Sensibility chapter XLIV

O

Obviate *verb*   Overcome.

"'Though with your usual anxiety for our happiness,' said Elinor, 'you have been obviating every impediment to the present scheme which occurred to you, there is still one objection which, in my opinion, cannot be so easily removed.'"

—*Sense & Sensibility* chapter XXV

"'That will obviate all difficulties you know; and from us I really think, my dear Jane, you can have no scruple to accept such an accommodation.'"

—*Emma* volume II chapter XVI

Orthography *noun*   The subset of grammar dealing with how words are spelled.

"He continued with her the whole time of her writing, to assist her

with his penknife or his orthography, as either were wanted . . ."
—Mansfield Park chapter II

P

Palliate *verb*   Cover with excuse; soften by favorable representations.

"His companions suggested only what could palliate imprudence, or smooth objections."

—Emma volume III chapter X

Panegyric *noun*   An expression of praise, as might be contained in a eulogy.

"'When you told Mrs. Bennet this morning that if you ever resolved upon quitting Netherfield you should be gone in five minutes, you meant it to be a sort of panegyric, of compliment to yourself—and yet what is there so very laudable in a precipitance which must leave very necessary business undone, and can be of no real advantage to yourself or anyone else?'"

—Pride & Prejudice chapter X

"This naturally introduced a panegyric from Jane on his diffidence, and the little value he put on his own good qualities."

—*Pride & Prejudice* chapter LV

Particularise, Particularize *verb*   Enumerate; specify; be particular.

"'I need not particularise.'"

—*Mansfield Park* chapter XLIV

Pattens *noun*   Wooden shoes bearing iron rings, worn over a woman's regular shoes to protect them from dirt.

". . . amidst the dash of other carriages, the heavy rumble of carts and drays, the bawling of newspapermen, muffin-men and milkmen, and the ceaseless clink of pattens . . ."

—*Persuasion* chapter XIV

Penury *noun*   Poverty; emptiness; lack of interesting or engaging contents.

"'And now to chuse the mortification of Mrs. Elton's notice and the penury of her conversation, rather than return to the superior companions who have always loved her with such real, generous affection.'"

—*Emma* volume II chapter XV

Pertinacity *noun*   1. Obstinacy; stubbornness. 2. Constancy; fidelity.

"The pertinacity of her friend seemed more than she could bear."

—*Emma* volume III chapter VI

Petulance *noun*   Sauciness or peevishness.

"It was gratitude; gratitude, not merely for having once loved her, but for loving her still well enough to forgive all the petulance and acrimony of her manner in rejecting him, and all the unjust accusations accompanying her rejection."

—*Pride & Prejudice* chapter XLIV

"Her continual disagreements with her mother, her rash squabbles with Tom and Charles, and petulance with Betsey, were at least so distressing to Fanny that, though admitting they were by no means without provocation, she feared the disposition that could push them to such length must be far from amiable, and from affording any repose to herself."

—*Mansfield Park* chapter XXXIX

Philippic *noun*   A vituperative tirade. (Developed in reference to the invective declamations of the Greek politician Demosthenes against King Philip II of Macedonia, whose expansion of his kingdom Demosthenes opposed.)

"The gruel came and supplied a great deal to be said—much praise and many comments—undoubting decision of its wholesomeness for every constitution, and pretty severe Philippics upon the many houses where it was never met with tolerably."

—Emma volume I chapter XII

Plait *noun*   A fold; a weave or braid.

"She was sitting by Edward, and in taking his tea from Mrs. Dashwood, his hand passed so directly before her, as to make a ring, with a plait of hair in the centre, very conspicuous on one of his fingers."

—Sense & Sensibility chapter XVIII

Pollard *noun*   A tree that has been lopped.

"'I do not often walk this way now,' said Emma, as they proceeded, 'but then there will be an inducement, and I shall gradually get intimately acquainted with all the hedges, gates, pools and pollards of this part of Highbury.'"

—Emma volume I Chapter X

Poplin *noun*   Stuff fabric made of silk and worsted; a wool that is thinner than cloth.

"'I have some notion of putting such a trimming as this to my white and silver poplin.'"

—Emma volume II chapter XVII

Postilion *noun*   The man who rides the first horse of a set of six pulling a coach, and guides the postchaise (a four-wheeled travelling carriage).

"'He meant, I believe,'" replied Jane, "to go to Epsom (the place where they last changed horses), see the postilions and try if anything could be made out from them. His principal object must be to discover the number of the hackney coach which took them from Clapham.'"

—*Pride & Prejudice* chapter XLVII

Practicable *adjective*   Capable of being performed.

"'How can you imagine such conduct practicable?'"

—*Emma* volume I chapter XVIII

Precipitance *noun*   Headlong hurry; rash haste.

"'. . . and yet what is there so very laudable in a precipitance which must leave very necessary business undone, and can be of no real advantage to yourself or anyone else?'"

—*Pride & Prejudice* chapter X

Prepossessed *adjective*   Possessing a first impression; filled with a rashly formed opinion; prejudiced in favor of or against something.

"'. . . Fanny and Mrs. Ferrars were both strongly prepossessed, that neither she nor her daughters were such kind of women as Fanny would like to associate with.'"

—*Sense & Sensibility* chapter XXXIII

"'. . . those to whom she endeavored to give pleasure were
prepossessed in her favour.'"
—Pride & Prejudice chapter XLIV

Prepossession *noun*   Prejudice; an opinion formed with
insufficient or incorrect information.

"'Pleased with the preference of the one, and offended by the
neglect of the other, on the very beginning of our acquaintance I
have courted prepossession and ignorance, and driven reason away,
where either were concerned.'"
—Pride & Prejudice chapter XXXVI

"'. . . Marianne's unhappy prepossession for that worthless
young man!'"
—Sense & Sensibility chapter XLV

"'. . . the picture will not be in Bond-street till just before he
mounts his horse to-morrow. It is his companion all this evening, his
solace, his delight. It opens his designs to his family, it introduces you
among them, it diffuses through the party those pleasantest feelings
of our nature, eager curiosity and warm prepossession.'"
—Emma volume I chapter VII

Prodigious *adjective*   Great, enormous, or in some other way
astonishing.

"'. . . in spite of what she had heard about the prodigious
accumulation of dirt in the course of that hour . . .'"
—Northanger Abbey chapter XI

"'Mr. Darcy is uncommonly kind to Mr. Bingley, and takes a prodigious deal of care of him.'"

—*Pride & Prejudice* chapter XXXIII

"'Five hundred pounds would be a prodigious increase to their fortunes!'"

—*Sense & Sensibility* chapter II

Profligacy *noun*　　　　The quality of being lost to all virtue and decency; the characteristic of being a shameless wretch.

"The extravagance and general profligacy which he scrupled not to lay at Mr. Wickham's charge, exceedingly shocked her; the more so, as she could bring no proof of its injustice."

—*Pride & Prejudice* chapter XXXVI

Promontory *noun*　　　　High land jutting out (usually into the sea), as in a cape or headland.

"'I can easily believe it to be full of rocks and promontories, grey moss and brush wood, but these are all lost on me. I know nothing of the picturesque.'"

—*Sense & Sensibility* chapter XVIII

Propitious *adjective*　　　　Favorable; kind.

"Her answer, therefore, was not propitious, at least not to Elizabeth's wishes, for she was impatient to get home."

—*Pride & Prejudice* chapter XII

Puppy *noun*   A contemptuous or reproachful term for a superficial, frivolous, silly young man.

"'An abominable puppy! You know who I mean' (nodding to her husband)."
>   —*Emma* volume III chapter VII

Puppyism *noun*   Extreme affectation.

"'I think him a very handsome young man, and his manners are precisely what I like and approve—so truly the gentleman, without the least conceit or puppyism.'"
>   —*Emma* volume III chapter I

Q

Quarto *noun*   A book made of paper sheets which are each folded to make four pages.

"... collecting and transcribing all the riddles of every sort that she could meet with, into a thin quarto of hot-pressed paper ..."
                    —*Emma* volume I chapter IX

Quiescent *adjective*   At rest; lying still.

"Lady Bertram was perfectly quiescent and contented ..."
                    —*Mansfield Park* chapter XXVI

R

Recantation *noun*   Retraction of a prior statement, or issuance of a new statement contradicting what was said prior.

". . . a recantation of past prejudices and errors . . ."
—*Emma* volume II chapter II

Ragout *noun*   A dish of stewed, highly seasoned meat. (French.)

". . . he was an indolent man, who lived only to eat, drink, and play at cards; who, when he found her to prefer a plain dish to a *ragout*, had nothing to say to her."
—*Emma* volume III chapter I

Repast *noun*   Meal; victuals; food.

"It was not four and twenty hours ago since they had met

there to the same repast, but in circumstances how different!"
—Northanger Abbey chapter XXVIII

Retrench *verb* 1. Trim away or cut off. 2. Live with less expense.

"'I know I cannot live as I have done, but I must retrench where I can, and learn to be a better manager.'"
—Mansfield Park chapter III

". . . he had gone so far as even as to say, 'Can we retrench?'"
—Persuasion chapter I

Riband, ribband *noun* A strip of silk worn for ornamentation.

"'Mr. Elton, I must beg leave to stop at your house, and ask your housekeeper for a bit of ribband or string, or any thing just to keep my boot on.'"
—Emma volume I chapter X

Rout-cake *noun* A rich cake, often made using almonds, usually consumed at an evening party.

"She was a little shocked at the want of two drawing rooms, at the poor attempt at rout-cakes, and there being no ice in the Highbury card-parties."
—Emma volume II chapter XVI

S

Scrubby *adjective*   Low; vile; worthless; dirty.

"'. . . I could not expect to be welcome in such a smart place
as that—poor scrubby midshipman as I am.'"
—*Mansfield Park* chapter XXV

Sprucebeer *noun*   Beer tinctured with branches of fir.

"'Mr. Knightley had been telling him something about
brewing spruce-beer, and he wanted to put it down . . .'"
—*Emma* volume III chapter IV

Spunging-house *noun*   A house where prisoners are sent before
being taken to debtor's prison; so-called due to the practice of bailiffs
of coercing money from them there.

"'Regard for a former servant of my own, who had since
fallen into misfortune, carried me to visit him in a spunging-house,

where he was confined for debt; and there, in the same house, under a similar confinement, was my unfortunate sister.'"

—Sense & Sensibility chapter XXXXI

Stricture *noun*   1. A stroke; a touch. 2. A slight touch upon a certain subject (as opposed to thorough discussion).

"'I was never more annoyed! The insipidity, and yet the noise—the nothingness, and yet the self-importance of these people! What would I give to hear your strictures on them!'"

—Pride & Prejudice chapter VI

Stupefaction *noun*   Torpor; dullness; insensibility; stupidity.

"At first, it was a sort of stupefaction; but every moment was quickening her perception of the horrible evil."

—Mansfield Park chapter XLVI

Supercilious *adjective*   Haughty; imperious; disdainful.

"For, though elated by his rank, it did not render him supercilious; on the contrary, he was all attention to everybody."

—Pride & Prejudice chapter V

T

Temporizing *verb*   Delaying; procrastinating; putting off.

"The shortness of his visit, the steadiness of his purpose in leaving them, originated in the same fettered inclination, the same inevitable necessity of temporizing with his mother."
—Sense & Sensibility chapter XIX

Tippet *noun*   Any cloth worn around the neck, such as a scarf or cravat.

"'Here is your tippet. Mrs. Weston begs you to put on your tippet. She says she is afraid there will be draughts in the passage . . .'"

—Emma volume III chapter II

Tressel *noun*   A temporary table; a moveable frame for resting things on. (Also called a "trestle" or "trestle table.")

"On one side was a table occupied by some chattering girls, cutting up silk and gold paper; and on the other were tressels and trays, bending under the weight of brawn and cold pies, where riotous boys were holding high revel . . ."

—Emma volume III chapter II

U

Umpire *noun*   A friend of two disputants, who arbitrates their disagreement.

"She had thought only of avoiding Captain Wentworth; but an escape from being appealed to as umpire was now added to the advantages of a quiet evening."

—Persuasion chapter IX

Understrapper *noun*   An inferior agent; an assistant.

"'No want of hands in our theatre, Miss Bertram. No want of understrappers . . .'"

—Mansfield Park chapter XIII

Unexampled *adjective*   Above imitation; impossible to copy.

"'I can no longer help thanking you for your unexampled

kindness to my poor sister.'"

—Pride & Prejudice chapter LVIII

Upbraid *verb*   Reproach; object contemptuously; charge with anything disgraceful.

"When she remembered the style of his address, she was still full of indignation; but when she considered how unjustly she had condemned and upbraided him, her anger was turned against herself . . ."

—Pride & Prejudice chapter XXXVII

"'But let me not interrupt you sir. You will not thank me for detaining you from the bewitching converse of that young lady, whose bright eyes are also upbraiding me.'"

—Pride & Prejudice chapter XVIII

V

Valetudinarian *noun*   A person who is weak, sickly, or infirm.

"The evil of the actual disparity in their ages (and Mr. Woodhouse had not married early) was much increased by his constitution and habits; for having been a valetudinarian all his life, without activity of mind or body, he was a much older man in ways than in years. . ."

—Emma volume I chapter I

Verdure *noun*   Green color.

"The five weeks which she had now passed in Kent had made a great difference in the country, and every day was adding to the verdure of the early trees."

—Pride & Prejudice chapter XXXV

Virulence *noun*   Mental poison; bitterness of temper.

"'And the lock of hair—that too I had always carried about me in the same pocket-book, which was now searched by Madam with the most ingratiating virulence,—the dear lock—all, every memento was torn from me.'"

—Sense & Sensibility chapter XLIV

Y

Yard-arm *noun*   The ends of the "yard" (the instrument which supports the sails), where the rigging is placed. Considered an extremely degrading punishment, being "run up the yard-arm" was a sentence administered to sailors derelict in the execution of their duty.

"". . . who was to tell it? Not I. I would as soon have been run up to the yard-arm.""

—*Persuasion* chapter

Younker *noun*   Young person; youngster.

""Ah! the peace has come too soon for that younker. Poor old Sir Archibald!""

—*Persuasion* chapter XVIII

ABOUT THE LEXICOGRAPHER

Emmalee Haskell is an historian and editor who lives and writes in the mountainous western U.S. A lifelong fan of dictionaries and history, she hopes that this book will be of use to those wishing to deepen their understanding of Austen and her world, increase their familiarity with particular meanings, or simply enjoy the colorful vagaries of linguistic history.